With This, I Release

Emma Raye

To those who believed in me

Thank you for giving me the strength to push forward,

when I felt I had none left

To those still struggling

This book is for you. The same scars we so desperately wish to forget, soon become the battle wounds we proudly wear. I believe in you, and with this book, I hope you learn to believe in yourself.

Contents:

Broken...... 5

Healing...... 42

Rising......88

Broken

I lie in bed

Staring at the popcorn ceiling

Thinking to myself

When will it go away?

The thought of not being enough

The need to feel anything other than my current

state of being

The ache of feeling so deeply broken

I wonder

When did it start?

With my first real heartbreak?

Or has it always been around?

Lingering about my mind

and body

Why is just now taking over my entire mind

I feel unable to breathe

Desperately just searching for a reason to keep

…living

-Heavy

Tears line the edges of my fragile face

I don't even try to wipe them away

I know they'll just reappear

With each tear

I feel the weight in which it takes to keep breathing

I can't get words out

So, I simply shut everyone out

I don't think they would understand how dark my

mind can get

The fact that when I am asleep

I feel most at peace

-Is it possible to feel at peace, when awake?

I found you in a time when I was already

so deeply shattered

I remember telling you

"just don't make me cry"

I know at the moment

it was sort of a joke

I knew you would at *some* point let me down

However

What I should have said was

Please don't make me fall

if you have no intention

of truly loving me

-You did the opposite

When you asked questions about my past

About the things that haunt my mind

The moments that drove my heart deep within my chest

I genuinely believed you were asking to know what not to repeat

To have a roadmap pointing out all the ways

how *not* to treat my already tortured soul

I never thought that months down the road

you would repeat those very same things

-Trust Issues

I step on the scale

It reads 154.6

I feel disgusted

I look at the extra skin on my body

as if it were a demeaning voice

Validating everything I've ever thought wrong

about myself

I don't eat much

But then again

I don't move much either

I long for the perfect body

It's the motivation to move that gets me

I repeat the words

"You're not worth it"

As I close my eyes

Only then drifting back into what I hope

will be a deep enough sleep

Deep enough to forget these thoughts

-Never enough for me

These unspoken words kill me

What might I say

if I had one more chance to speak with you?

Words run races around my mind

Tears rush out of my eyes like waterfalls

Bringing me

directly to my knees

Taking the last of my energy

As if they're pulling me under the ocean tide

Gasping for air once more

I scream

WHY?!

-Unspoken

There is no such thing as closure

When you truly love someone

When they break your heart

No reasoning will ever seem good enough

Because you truly would have done anything to keep them

To think of them giving up for any reason

Just seems insensitive

But the truth is

Sometimes two people are just not meant to be

You will hurt

You will scream

You will cry

You will spend nights upon nights wondering

Just wondering desperately what went wrong

Until

One morning you will wake up, and be okay

The sun will rise

You will see the beauty of living again

You will see it all without that person you so desperately held onto

I know it hurts

-Please just hold on

You say you don't want me

But the moment the sun sets beneath the horizon

You call for me

As if your words did not just grip onto my soul

And drive me deep into my bedsheets

As if your words had no effect

You continuously treat them as if they are

momentary lapses in judgement

Dismissing all responsibility

When the moonlight shines

You act as if I am the only thing you'd ever need

Only then caressing my mind with your mysterious

Yet charming ways

They whisper "I need you"

Until the moment that dawn breaks

You once again raise the stakes

Spitting out words that mutter

"I can't do this"

-I never learn

Never thought we'd end up like this

Never did I believe we'd be strangers again

We threw it away

How do you go from long nights

Music on repeat

No sleep

To missed calls

Left on read

It's draining figuring out how we let this become so dead

Maybe it was you

Maybe it was me

When I think back on those days

Maybe I'm just not seeing clearly

I thought we had it all

In the blink of an eye

We fell to the bottom

Sinking beneath the rubble

But still, when I look back on the good

I seem to forget the bad

Is my vision really that foggy?

-Rose colored glasses?

My biggest regret is you

To this day

I still don't know

If it's because of loving you

Or letting you go

-Will I ever know?

You drunkenly spit out

"maybe you're just a warm body"

Those words follow me

Like ghosts

searching for a meaning

Is that really all I am?

After everything?

I responded saying

"I can't compete with history"

You respond

calling me to come over

As I write this,

I still can't fathom why I did

Why I still would

Those six words hit me like a bullet to the chest

And yet

I *still* stuck the key in the ignition

I *still* walked to your front steps

I *still* held you through the night

I *still* don't understand why I wouldn't take those actions back

Even after finding out that you still had feelings for her

I still tried to make you see

that we were worth it

That you were worth it

Countless nights

I cried myself to sleep

Wondering how I could have been so blind

I hated myself so deeply

for just being human

I had never looked in the mirror so often

Utterly disgusted with just me

Consistently wondering how something that started out so beautiful

Could turn to something so ugly

So confusing

I lost myself in the maze of us

I abandoned my self-worth

Simply trying to put the pieces together

I'm not sure I'll ever love that way again

To give my heart so freely

Despite knowing the consequences

The consequences of never get it back again

The loneliness I was bound to feel

every time it would abruptly come to a halt

My willingness to keep going back

Out of pure love

And a lack of self-worth

I don't think my heart would survive a second round

Not with anyone

-My heart is tired

I never understood how you could just change your mind

So quickly

Like a change in the wind

I understood your confusion

Or your need to not look like a fool

Your willingness to toss my soul into the nearest trash can

Whenever you felt it was too much

As if you had the ability to push a button and feel nothing

That is what I cannot fathom

My emotions are so concrete

Much like your commitment to service

I suppose it's because that act of service doesn't

Require a state of vulnerability

Only black and white commitment

to the fulfillment of a mission

-Questions

I miss you so much

I don't want to

I want to hate you

I want to never want to speak with you again

I long to look at your face

and feel nothing

Yet, I still feel everything

I feel your hands running down my back

I feel your mouth two inches from mine

I feel you asking me to come closer

I wish I'd known

when you were spewing those pretty lies

They were the last I'd hear

I didn't know it was goodbye

What's sad

is if I had known it was the last time

I would have held on so much tighter

I would have held your gaze longer

Because all I want now

Is to feel you again

To touch you once more

To whisper face to face

Underneath covers

It beats my hears black and blue

-I hate myself for wanting you as deeply as I do

Walls

I've got so many walls

I keep them higher than the kite I flew as a kid

I refuse to bring them down

They're wrapped in barbwire

Forever protecting my already broken heart

from completely shattering

If you dare to break through them

You will get hurt

My brain seems to reject what's good for it

I long for the day my walls feel at ease enough to

be lowered

Sadly

That day has not come

-Please don't get close

We weren't built to last

But I wish we were

The way we collided at night

Made me feel as if we may just get it right

Instead

We're oil and water

A flame to a match

The perfect storm at times

A tornado destroying everything

that may come across her path

Still, that look in your eyes

To this day

has strings wrapped around my fragile heart

-Inevitable failure

When I was younger

all I wanted to do was roam

I lived in paper dreams

Never wanting to be home

Longing for the day I'd leave

Create my own happily ever after

Pack up my things and never look back

In my mind

I'd go to brighter places

Maybe somewhere by the water

Somewhere with kind faces

Anywhere I didn't constantly feel on edge

Happiness was the goal

But what is happiness?

Somehow it always feels as if it's locked in a glass case

Am I too messed up now?

At times I wish I could plow through a brick wall

Maybe then I could find what I'm looking for

Maybe on the other side would be the key to it all

The key to what I've been desperately searching for

-Do I even know what I'm searching for?

How did you make me feel so understood?

Like anything I wanted to say

I just could

You mended me to my core

I don't presume you even knew

Not the extent to which your existence alone

calmed my entire soul

Maybe that was your role

To awaken my soul

To enlighten my mind

Just for it all to come crashing back down

-I always wanted more

I knew the moment I saw you

That I had fallen for you

Maybe it was the collision of two tired souls

I had never been one for open emotions

But with you

It all just felt so new

-Blue

I have many tattoos

But there is one that I wander back to

More than the others

The one that keeps my heart in a bind

Perhaps even by a chokehold

It is the invisible thread between two souls

The funny thing is

I don't know that it ever held as much meaning before

As it does today

The last string of faith I desperately keep close

-We'll meet again, right?

Before it was tumultuous

It was sweet

Before the rain

It was nothing but clear skies

Before resentment

There was love

So much love

Before dishonesty

I had never trusted anyone more

Before letting you go

I wanted nothing more than to hold on

The before is what makes this after

So. Damn. Hard.

-Before

I look in the mirror

I pick my body apart

I think about what I could change if I could

I ask myself why I can't just be skinny

I see every flaw from my head to my toes

I tell myself if I had that perfect skin

That perfect body

I'd be loved

Maybe if I were more tan

If my stomach were flatter

Maybe then I could really be loved

Before I march on with my day

I look one last time

I ask myself

"When will everything I already am, be good enough for just me"

-Self Love

My walls did not get this tall overnight

They did not become this sturdy with a moon's passing

No

In fact, they grew their strength over years

They have kept me alive

Protected me from potentially agonizing pain

My walls are 5'8 in height

150 lbs in approximate weight

They are every bit of my being

My walls are all I know now

To think of them being broken down

Means to think of them being shattered

To think of my walls being opened

Not only makes my mind implode with intrusive thoughts

But

Reminds me that my already fragile heart could once more

Be battered

To be Forgotten

Abandoned

-What I tell myself

My mind is like a tree in the winter

My core is strong

Sturdy

My branches though

The components of which my body comprises

They are brittle

The center of my being

I wish to bring back to life

To have the color reignited

My zest for life

Where did it go?

The way I would effortlessly reach for more

With my summer branches

They were so green

They were watered with life

Strengthened by comfort

Stood tall with confidence

Until much like winter

Certain events hardened my core

Dimmed the light of all color

My deepest roots are gasping for breath

Desperately wishing not only the warmth

But for the color to reappear

-Where did you go?

The sand

The moon

You

I had everything

Everything I wanted

Right beside me

On one lonesome night

-Words for You

Green Eyes

Sunset pools

When I saw you

I saw the sun

Burning so bright

Green has left me

Mesmerized

Your eyes

That's all it took

For my entire being

To know

I feel

Safe…

-Thank You

I would rather suffer all my worst hangovers

All at once

Than to spend one more minute

Drowning in thoughts of you

-Where's the alcohol?

You say

"Just tell me what you need, and I'll tell you if I can do it or not"

The problem is

All I need

Is you

-Wrong Path

If I could think of a way to not think of you

I would

But until I'm blessed with amnesia

You'll be the start to my day

And every thought after

Until my head down I lay

-Heartache

I've always told myself

I'm avoiding commitment

How is it that one who is so scared of commitment

Has nine tattoos?

No really,

Nine times I decided

"This is better than a relationship"

Thinking that was avoiding getting hurt

As the needle jams into my skin 949 times

-Make it make sense

For as long as I can remember

I have felt ashamed

Of my body

For I've believed it is not enough

I see every flaw when I glance in the mirror

Of my mind

For I've believed it does not measure up

Unable to be understood

Of my heart

For I've believed it is too large

After all,

Who could love a heart that feels so intensely?

-Thoughts that linger in my mind

Healing

At times my memories leave me with a warmth in my heart

A deeper smile for the moment

Other times

My memories take me back to feeling as if the sun has set

And will not rise

Furthermore

The memories that leave the crinkle in between my eyes

The fire within my soul

Those are the memories I choose not to bury

The ones I soar back into my mind for the most

For those are the memories that keep my wild heart

…..Going

-Lifeline

Rain Clouds

These clouds keep a close eye over my head

They pull me under and drown me out

These clouds seem to follow wherever I may be

The rain pours

It seems as if it will never let up

I start to feel as if I am drowning

Out of nowhere it stops

The clouds begin to part

The rain ceases

At this moment

I see the rainbow they've created

My mind is awakened

I suddenly realize

All darkness eventually leads to light

In time the dark fades

The colors begin to creep back in

Making life again

One beautiful mess

In moments when I find myself breaking

I am reminded of how far I've come

I have yet to reach a feeling of peace

However, I no longer fall asleep wishing to not wake up

That must mean something right?

I'm learning to not be so hard on myself

To appreciate what I do have

Instead of what I do not

I have a long way to go

But the colors are beginning to look brighter

For me

In this moment

That is all I could ask

-Small Things

In case you were wondering

I live life more freely now

I laugh more

I feel more

However, it is in the moments where I flash back

To just sitting next to you

Those little flashes bring back every emotion

And all at once

I feel everything

I refrain from doing so most times

But I can't stop my mind from wandering

Into those moments I go

Crashing into a state of vulnerability

I try to stop it

At times though

It's just not possible

You were the sunlight in darkness

The sweet before it turned bitter

- I remember the good and bad

You'll never understand the hurt you put me through

The sleepless nights

Crying until I felt sick

Not knowing if I was ever going to feel okay again

The agony of not being able to forget your touch

You'll never know

When you let me go

I spend months hiding beneath bedsheets

Wondering if I had done one thing differently

If it would have changed anything

I lost so much time

Just searching for a reason

Desperately wishing for the changing of the season

Until one morning it just clicked

-Maybe we just weren't meant to be

Will I ever get over what we had?

I truly don't know

There are times when I feel the possibility of love again

Shortly after, I see your eyes

How they were the only ones my soul seemed to understand

Furthermore, the ones that understood my soul

All the way down to its core

I thought I'd known love before

Until the day you entered my life

That was the day I knew nothing would ever be the same

Now I begin to wonder

Maybe I was meant to live a life of purpose

Instead of a life of love

Maybe I'm just coping

All I know is that you're the one my heart wants to come home to

My heart still wants the long nights

The tears

The comfort

The "come closer"

There isn't a day where it doesn't relentlessly

Lead right back to you

-Wants VS Needs

I'm beginning to let your memory go

I wish I could say I'm elated

But I'm not

You were the sweater I never wanted to take off

The color I could have made my eternity

The laugh I had memorized

I weep at the thought of forgetting it all

I wish I could stop it

But the need to feel something other pain

Other than tears streaming down my dry cheeks

Has now overcome the will to not let you go

-I will always miss you, even in letting you go

I'm bound by the soul that holds my heart

Knowing it will never be mine again

The possibility of falling for another

the way I fell for you

May perhaps be what keeps my tired soul alive

-Once in a lifetime?

I'm allowed to hurt

To feel my pain

To let myself fall

I'm allowed to break into a million pieces

Don't you dare tell me I can't

Not when I spend months validating your feelings

This is me healing

I will not bury my emotions

Only to find that they come back twice as strong

down the ever-winding road

I will feel my emotions

I will let them pour out

I will work through them

And I will not feel bad about it

-Don't tell me I can't

On the nights you weren't with me

I knew she was around

I can't say I wasn't expecting it

I heard her name as you muttered

"I don't want anything with anyone right now"

I heard the exception in that sentence

I do regrettably wish you the best

I achingly still want you to be happy

However

Don't think it doesn't break me to know that I was just a stop

A stop along the way in your healing journey

While you made me face plant into what would begin to be mine

I loved you with my whole heart

So instead of being angry

Instead of remaining bitter

I will just say

I hope she makes your soul feel at home

-The way I thought our souls were home

Sometimes I think I'm just bitter

Then I remember the softness I feel from a warm touch

I remember the look and feeling of being loved

I then remember gentle words

Kind hearts

It is in this moment that I remember

I am not bitter

I am just human

I am too searching for the meaning of my life

Even through all the mazes

I suppose that these soft moments

Awaken my soul to realize through the light

And dark

I am simply,

Just me

Just a soul

-Scary

There was a time when he was good

But not good enough to make me stay

You may say that's crazy

You may ask why

The truth is

No matter how much love you have

You can't force a puzzle piece to fit

Where it doesn't belong

You can't breathe life into a dying flower

Expecting it to bloom again

At times you must make a choice

Not only for yourself

But for them also

-I'm Sorry

If you're not careful

While healing

You will hurt others

If you do not solely search for healing

Within yourself

You will cause pain in others

Just to fill the void within yourself

Healing takes time

You must nurture your own soul

Before inviting another in

I have been the one to hurt the heart of another

And I have been the one who has been hurt

Both times

It was due to a deep need to feel understood

without finding the understanding first

within myself

-Heal within first

Truthfully

I always believed he could find someone better

To fit the mold

To love him better

The way in which he needed

Our love was so different

My love is ocean waves

Calming

Yet

Consistently ready to passionately crash with the sand

It takes a deeper understanding for my love

His love was blue skies

Sunshine

Never knowing darkness

Always needing the bright light

Lightning striking if it were anything other than perfect

However

My heart belongs to the storm

The gravity that the moon gives to the ocean waves

That is what inspires the music within my soul

That is type of love that my heart has to offer

A type in which he could not understand

-I can't apologize for my type of love

The stars give me hope on a dark night

They remind me that no matter how far

No matter how distant

I can still reach them

They give me hope

They remind me that with enough persistence

They are always reachable

The motivation they bring to my soul

The fire they ignite within

The way the moon touches the waves

Pulls them in and out

Ever so gently

Yet

Commanding them to move

That is that type of love I crave

-Move me

My wings are deeply tattered

Yet time and time again

I still find the strength to fly

-Still alive

I have only been merely surviving

In a world

Where I am meant to thrive

-It's okay to start over

I tried to work it away

I tried to drink it away

Each time

I plummeted farther down

Into a deep

Dark rabbit hole

Of numbed emotions

-You must feel it all, to work through it all

For me,

You were all night phone calls

A light night drive to slip under covers

Tangled bedsheets

You were a sweet smile, with a hesitant wild side

My best day

My worst night

The songs I kept on repeat

I was wrapped so tightly around your finger

I neglected to live for myself

I will never get over just the sound of your voice

Could bring me to my knees

However, now I know that

I was meant to live

Happy and free

To find the peace in being alone

Not desperately waiting at a broken streetlight

for someone who would never show

For you, I was a stop along the way

A comfortable place in which your head could lay

Only until you found a new direction

In which you could sway

-Tortured Souls

I wanted to hear you say that you loved me

I just wanted to hear it

Just to know that even if we couldn't work

You loved me

It would have made my love for you feel worthwhile

Like I was less of a fool

It wasn't the ending that shook me to my core

It was knowing how easily you made the decision

Over and over again

I tried to make you feel loved

Like you were enough

The countless nights that I held you through your pain

And in return

After everything

When I asked you what this was to you

All you said was

"I don't think I couldn't have learned to breathe again without it"

I don't know if that makes me angry, or happy for you

As if all I was here for

Was to bring you back to the surface again

While I was slowly sinking down

With what felt like anchors tied to my feet

Drowning

You learned to breathe again

While I learned what I meant to feel darkness again

-I just wanted to hear you say you loved me

Time does not heal all wounds

Time does not close the scar on your heart

Or stop the bleeding

Time does magically recreate the spark within

Time Is not a reset button

On the contrary

Time does make you realize your worth

That your scars are beautiful

Time does lessen the visibility of your deep wounds

It does refresh the mind

Time may not cure

But times does help you to

-Keep going

I always believed that love should be passionate

On fire

I wanted to think It was as if running full force into another

With no thought of repercussion

The truth though

Is that love is like a Sunday morning

Birds Chirping

Waterfalls flowing

True love awakens the soul

It brings peace to not only the heart

But the mind

I know this

Because I had the chance to love you

Although in the end, loving you was breaking me

I can still remember the feeling of meeting you

The moment in which my entire being sighed

I felt a relief in that one moment

Like no other

-Forever in my mind

I long to feel like chamomile tea

Consistently calm

Not too sweet

Yet not bitter

I would say I have instead been like that of black coffee

Energizing

But bitter within

Used to keep others lifted

I want to be the center of warmth

For me

You see

Coffee is a pick me up

It's strong

But the inevitable crash is stronger

Chamomile tea is loving

Holds you from the first sip

Only needed to feel at ease

After a day of heavy

Rough seas

The sand

The moon

You

I had everything

Everything I wanted

Right beside me

On one lonesome night

-Words for You

I always hated eye contact

It made my hands clam up

My heart race

Always made me feel vulnerable

Too vulnerable

I never felt safe longing into another's eyes

That is

Until I met you

It was like looking into open fields

One look jumpstarted my soul

As if it were set on fire

With one match

My love for you grew

-I always hated eye contact

I heard one of our songs today

Almost like a sign to remember the good

It went a bit like *this*

"I know a place we can go"

"Where everybody gonna lay down their weapon"

"Just give me trust, and watch what'll happen"

The tears streamed down my face all at once

For the first time in months

I listened to it all the way through

I let the lyrics sink into my soul

Completely taking over me

For all of 3 minutes and 50 seconds

I have kept that song tucked away

Buried beneath the rubble of us

In doing so

I forgot how much it meant to me

And in listening to it

I was reminded how I have done the same to the memory of us

I think you'll always be a part of me

Perhaps not in the way I had hoped

But in a shapeshifting

Character building sort of way

I had wished we'd be our own greatest adventure

Like that of traveling to your favorite place

Except that favorite place was us

I thought of us as home

You were my comfort

The silver lining in a whole lot of bad

The moments I looked forward to

Time and time again

I just wish it had been the same for you

You were my home

But I was not yours

I've found trying to block you out only makes it worse

It begins to feel like the knife that just keeps twisting

So instead

I remember that there is purpose in everything

I choose now to think back on you fondly

Knowing that I could not have grown without you

Even with the downpour of emotions

The tears that still unexpectedly flood my eyes

I choose to remember

That without the rain

Flowers could not bloom

-I choose

Sometimes I think about the choices we make

As individuals

As human beings

we stumble through life doing what we think is best

Spending our days struggling to fully live

While also trying to survive the long nights

I wonder if we knew the difference between important

and not important

If we would choose differently

Would we take that opportunity, despite not having any backup plan

if we knew that it would work out in the end?

Would we let go of our fears sooner

if we knew that 6 months later, we'd be better for it?

Or would we still stay put

in our self-made boxes of comfort?

Each time I've convinced myself something was

too far out of reach

I've found later

that it was always within my reach

It was I that persuaded myself otherwise

So, I pose this question

If you knew that everything would eventually turn in your favor

Would you take the risk?

-10:37 PM

I'm not sure I will ever get the answer to this

But do you think we could have worked?

I don't say that lightly

I know the time, and place

was quite literally impossible

From my perspective

I think that is what tore us in half

The doubts

The fears

The insecurities

We went from something beautiful

To that of much like a sink hole

I do wonder sometimes though

Do you think we could have worked?

-I may very well never know

I'm learning that we all have baggage

Sure, for some it's more like a carry on

Light weight

Manageable

More like deep emotions in the back of one's mind

For others it's more like that of checked luggage

with too much weight

The one where you're told if you do not part

with some of it

You cannot go through

The carry-on baggage is what those with check luggage wish to be like

The feeling of being free to roam about

Not having to constantly pick and choose what can stay

And what must go

With that though

At the end of the day

It is all still baggage

-We are all relatable in some way, or another

I've started keeping a picture of younger me

I keep her close

As a reminder of how far

we've come

When I start to criticize myself

I pull out this one picture

Reminding myself that even if we are not where

we yet want to be

Still, we have come a long way from where we once were

I tell myself all the validating words

The comforting phrases

Everything I craved as a young girl

Only then realizing once more

That deep validation comes from within

-I have the power

For the longest time

I believed that to be happy

You had to have it all together

Married by 22

The dream job by 24

Little feet running around by 26

With this mindset

I truly believe I have held myself back

Happiness is not something you find in someone

else

It's not a feeling any job can give you

Furthermore

You certainly can't raise happy

children

while still holding a deep void within

Coming to terms with this has been monumental

Not only for my mental health

But for my heart, as well

-Shapeshifting

I don't look back on my childhood much

Not the bad anyways

I never thought it would do any good to revisit it all

The feeling of being so helpless

As a child I knew I was missing something

Maybe a sense of comfort

Or stability

I've always chosen to not think about it

My parents both separately did the best they could

With what they had

In healing though

I've come to the realization that it is necessary

Those same moments I refuse to look back on

Are the same ones I know are holding me back

-Take the leap

There's this little girl inside of me

She is *afraid*

She is *insecure*

She is *unsure*

I've found this little girl has seeped into my adulthood

The motivation to find peace within

Has led me on a journey to the past

If the little girl within in me is not healed

I cannot expect to ever feel at peace

Not fully

So, I deep dive into the unknown

Hoping just maybe this leads me back home

To my true self

-The Healed Version

When I had my heart broken for the first time

I couldn't help but wonder

Why it felt so familiar

The truth is that it felt familiar

Because it was familiar

Way too familiar

-In an effort to move past it all

Let me first say

I love my parents deeply

They both loved me in their own way

However

As I was growing up

So were they

My mom was battling her own demons

My dad was battling his

Both fighting those battles in different ways

My mom filling voids with less than worthy people

My dad filling voids with never ending work

I've had a hard time writing something I know they will read

Due to how much I know it will hurt them

I just hope they know

I love them

But I am also now trying to fill my voids

In a different way

-Finding peace in empty moments

Growing up with divorced parents

is not uncommon

But no one ever talks about the constant tug-of-war

feeling this causes

within a child

Especially when the two

are not exactly on friendly terms

Feeling like I was never at ease

Feeling like it was a constant game of who was the

better parent

Feeling like I just wanted to be comforted

Most of all

The feeling of just wanting them to be present

-Loved, but not feeling loved

I realized I was following in the footsteps of my parents

When I began drinking when I felt uneasy

Or uncomfortable

When I felt more at home at work

Than in my actual home

When I found myself avoiding my own emotions for the comfort of others

I don't want to repeat the mistakes of my family's past

I would rather follow in their good steps

I would rather become the healed version of them

-Breaking the cycle

Rising

Water the roots

Pick the weeds

Bloom with the sun

Rise within

-You are the flower

I have spent my entire life standing up for everyone

but myself

25 years of taking care of everyone's emotions

but my own

Those days are over

It is exhausting

I will not shrink myself

for the comfort of anyone else's ego

I refuse to think of myself as less than

for creating necessary boundaries

I will not let my emotions be buried beneath the surface

just because that is what was done before me

I will take care of my well being

I will fight for myself

I will take time off for myself

And I will not feel bad about it

-Rise

When I began my healing journey

It was all about who hurt me

The anger I felt in letting my guard down

Only for it to be abandoned

Left in the dust

Through healing I have found

It had nothing to do with who hurt me

And everything to do with why it was hurting me

Only then could I even begin to truly heal

-Taking my power back

I admired traits in others

that were always in me

I despised myself for what I was not

When I had the power all along

I choose what I am

And what I'm not

What traits I posses

And those I do not

-You have a choice

My childhood was undoubtably chaotic

We went through a lot together

Again though

I struggle with writing about it

Because I don't wish it had been any different

I know the "American Dream"

is the perfect family

Is any family 100% perfect?

I have found that all that glitters

Is not gold

Even the happiest of families have their secrets

Would I really be who I am today

without it all?

The good, and the bad

are what mold a human

Not just the shiny

But the gritty

as well

When my mother begins to apologize

for the past

I wish she could understand

I do not hold resentment

We are all growing

She was growing

How beautiful

to be able to watch your mother

become everything she hoped she could be

How inspiring to see your own mother

win her battles

I would consider myself lucky

to be half the woman she has become

To hold half the strength she does

-It is okay

My father

regrets not being around more

He regrets the time spent at work

That could have been spent with us

What he doesn't know

Is I admire him

His tenacity to provide

The way he still calls me his baby girl

No matter how many mistakes I make

The way in which he says he's proud of me

No matter what

Because he never heard those words

I admire him

-Again, it is okay

If I were to ever see you again

I would smile

Knowing I had the chance to love so

deeply

The chance to feel brighter than all the stars in the

sky combined

For a moment

My eyes may well up

In knowing those days

are now long over

As the tears stream down my face

I would be grateful to have had the chance

To feel a love so pure

So real

To see colors so vividly

-Here's to remembering the good

In healing

I've found

We do not always keep those we love

Not forever anyways

But we do get to keep the memories

We get to keep the growth that follows

The lessons learned from each painstaking experience

-What keeps my spirit alive

Repeat after me

I am the key to my own happiness

I am the strength needed to weather all storms

I am the inspiration to be everything I desire

I am and will always be

all that I need

My roots may run dry

But it is I that waters them

I am enough

-Words of Affirmation

There is a flaw in society

when it comes to our youth

We teach them about fairytales

and happily ever after's

long before we ever teach them about the

importance of self-care

Before even inspiring the need for inner peace

I mutter that this is a flaw

because they grow up thinking that happiness is

found in almost anything, or anyone

but themselves

They enter society confusing boundaries

with being impolite

How do we expect them to grow up knowing their

own worth

if we are showing them everything but that?

How can we expect them to be healthy adults

if we are not even teaching them how to be?

-Our youth deserves more

There's this reoccurring dream I have

I'm sprinting

I keep looking back

Gasping for breath

In the middle of a crisp and cold forest

Searching for something behind me

I look forward

just long enough to keep running

Before suddenly snapping my head back around

to what's behind me

In this dream it always ends with me falling

Right before waking

I've realized maybe the reason this dream is

reoccurring

Is because I allow my past to consume me

Constantly searching for what is

and always will be

behind me

Relentlessly looking to rewrite things that are

already set in stone

I feel for the young ones

being told they are old souls

The ones that had to grow up to fast

Only to find in adulthood

that they must grow

all over again

In a completely different way

Old souls are just children

that had no choice

but to be mature enough to survive

Old souls bury their own feelings

to help others with theirs

Only to find years later they now must

search for protection of their own peace

Old souls forget that boundaries are necessary

And okay

They spend their childhood looking after others

Until one day

they wonder who is looking after them

Not in a financial way

Not in a roof over their head sort of way

But in a self-care

Creating healthy habits

Sort of way

Knowing that the word no is okay

Protecting their space

Living without chaos sort of way

-I feel for the old souls

I will always have me

In learning this

I have learned

To protect my space

At all costs

-Self Awareness

There is strength in learning

Strength behind scars

At times

They need to be re-opened

To be felt once more

As a reminder

In knowing

That no matter what

We will make it through

We will heal

We will rise

-Deep Roots

I have yearned for miracles

I only could have found

Within myself

-Dig Deep

I find comfort in words

When I cannot verbally express them

My pen will express them all

Onto the paper my emotions spill

As if my mind were a waterfall

Knowing exactly where to go

-Watering the soul

I am worth it

With all my imperfections

I will always be worth it

-How was I so blind?

I think the reality of growing up

Is realizing that you must be

your own safety net

It's coming to terms with home

being somewhere

you build within yourself

You see

If you are your own home

No one can take it from you

No one can abandon *your* home

It is only you

that has that power

When you begin to think of yourself as home

you work to protect that home

Protecting the home within

is how inner peace is discovered

They say home is where the heart is

But we forget to remember our own hearts in that sentence

Finding home within your own soul

may by far

be the most challenging task you will face

But it is a journey worth going on

-Home

I am far from where I wish to be

But I am getting there

I find peace in knowing

just how far I've come

I went from holding onto

the thought of living

By only an ever-weakening thread

To thriving on the thought of

What comes next

Looking back

At one point

That is all I could have ever asked for

-Growing

I once felt ashamed of the skin I live in

I once felt disgusted with the woman I saw

in the mirror

I once refused to speak with conviction

Now I am proud of the body I call home

Now I am amazed with the woman in the mirror

Staring beautifully back at me

Now I refuse to speak

with anything but conviction

-The other side

With these words

I wish for you to find solace

A kindred peace in knowing

I too

Have felt your pain

With these words

I pray you take yourself

to higher levels of understanding

Only then realizing you

And only you

Have had the power all along

-Believe in yourself

Find peace in the now

Not the past

Not the future

But the now

Find the beauty

in the everyday struggle

The weeds that just won't go away

The clouds that refuse to part

The traffic at the worst possible time

Once you find solace in the now

Everything else begins to seem that much lighter

-Peace

Rising does not mean setbacks cease

to exist

Rising does not mean the pain stops

Rising by no means takes away all fear

Rising does mean blooming

despite it all

Rising means accepting life

in every form it has to offer

Rising means being who you wish to

without allowing voices to hold you back

-You are worth it

With this, I release shame

With this, I release not feeling

good enough

With this, I release negative body image

With this, I release the hold of my past

With this, I release any thought of not

being capable

Not being strong enough

…to bloom

-With This, I Release

Made in the USA
Columbia, SC
21 March 2024